Bloc Politics at the United Nations

The African Group

Isaac N. Endeley

UNIVERSITY PRESS OF AMERICA,® INC.
Lanham • Boulder • New York • Toronto • Plymouth, UK

Library of Congress Control Number: 2009924564
ISBN: 978-0-7618-4558-4 (paperback : alk. paper)
eISBN: 978-0-7618-4559-1

Contents

Illustrations

Part One

THE THREE AFRICAN GROUPS

INTRODUCTION

The year 1960 is often described as "the year of Africa" because in that year alone, 16 of the former colonial territories on the continent became independent, sovereign States and acquired legal personalities of their own. Those States were: Benin (known at the time as Dahomey), Burkina-Faso (Upper Volta), Cameroon, the Central African Republic, Chad, Congo (Belgian), Congo (French), Côte d'Ivoire (Ivory Coast), Gabon, Madagascar, Mali, Niger, Nigeria, Senegal, Somalia, and Togo. As a symbol of their newfound status, all of these States rushed to become Members of the United Nations (UN). However, as both the newer and the older States embarked on the path of nation-building, it became apparent to many of them that they lacked the means individually to accomplish their goals and to cater to the needs of their populations. They easily realized that it was only by coming together and pooling their resources that they would be able to make any significant headway into the international political and economic scene. That realization can be characterized as the genesis of the movement towards continental integration and the establishment of common political and legal institutions (Endeley 1998).

Unfortunately, the overwhelming scope of the colonial experience had left Africa very severely fragmented both in the geo-political sense—as evidenced by the multitude of mini-States established on the continent—and also ideologically. From an ideological perspective, not only did the prevailing Cold War context create a significant cleavage along the East-West allegiances, but also the dissimilar and competing colonial legacies bequeathed to Africa by the Belgian, British, and French colonizers led to the establishment of separate

1

communities based on linguistic and cultural affinities. (The Portuguese colonies would only acquire their independence in the late 1970s following the "Velvet Revolution" in Lisbon and bloody liberation struggles in Africa.) Because of these rifts, there emerged on the continent three distinct groupings of States during the early 1960s. They were known by the names of the cities in which they were formally constituted: the Brazzaville Group, the Casablanca Group, and the Monrovia Group.

Chapter One

The Brazzaville Group

The first of the African groups to be formally constituted was the Brazzaville Group. It comprised some fifteen former French and Belgian colonies that opted to remain closely allied to the West in general and to France in particular (Hippolyte). This group was noted at the United Nations for voting in the same way as France on almost every important question, as demonstrated by the high voting correlations between them from 1960 to 1963 (Newcombe and Wert). On the two crucial questions of how to deal with the Congolese and Algerian crises, for instance, this group of States generally supported the position of France and other Western powers at the UN.

During its short existence it also succeeded in establishing a solid institutional framework, which included such key structures as the Organization of African and Malagasy Economic Cooperation (better known by its French acronym, OAMCE) and the African and Malagasy Union (UAM) (Chronologie 1961a, 1961b). The OAMCE, which was based in Yaoundé, Cameroon, was primarily a forum for economic cooperation while the UAM, with its headquarters at Cotonou, Guinea, was mainly a political institution. The Brazzaville Group also set up a Permanent Secretariat at the United Nations in New York to assist in the harmonization of the Member States' foreign policies and to help coordinate their diplomatic activities (UAM Establishes New York Office). This institutional framework gave the group the appearance of being more formal and more efficient than its two rival organizations. It also held "summit meetings" more frequently than the other groups of African States. (See Table 1.1.)

Following the creation of the Organization of African Unity (OAU) in 1963, the Brazzaville Group decided to dissolve itself in the interest of

3

Table 1.1. Summit Meetings of the African Groups (1958–1963)

	1958	1959	1960	1961	1962	1963
Brazzaville Group			Abidjan, Côte d'Ivoire October 24–26 ************ Brazzaville, Congo (French) December 15–19	Yaoundé, Cameroon March 26–28 ************ Antananarivo, Madagascar September 7–12	Bangui, Central African Republ. March 25–27 ************ Libreville, Gabon September 12–14	Ouagadougou, Upper Volta March 10–14
Casablanca Group	Accra, Ghana April 15–22			Casablanca, Morocco January 4–7	Cairo, Egypt June 15–18	
Monrovia Group				Monrovia, Liberia May 8–12	Lagos, Nigeria January 25–30	
Organization of African Unity (OAU)						Addis Ababa, Ethiopia May 22–25

Source: *Africa Report*, Vol. 8, No. 6, June 1963, p. 32 (adapted).

continental integration (Chronologie 1963). It even agreed to let the new Pan-African body assume control of its New York office. However, the transition did not come easily and the Francophone States continued their close and exclusive relations with each other within the framework of the new African and Malagasy Union for Economic Cooperation (UAMCE), established in Dakar, Senegal in March 1964 (Chronologie 1964). This close collaboration was further extended a year later with the creation of the Organization of African and Malagasy Cooperation (OCAM), in Nouakchott, Mauritania in February 1965 (Chronologie 1965).

Chapter Two

The Casablanca Group

At the other end of the ideological spectrum was the Casablanca Group, made up of the more radical African States that elected to sever all ties with the West and to forge very strong relations with the East bloc in general and the Soviet Union in particular (Amate 191; Boutros-Ghali 13). The Members of this faction included Ghana under Kwame Nkrumah, Guinea under Sékou Touré, Morocco under King Hassan II, as well as Mali, the United Arab Republic (Egypt), and the Provisional Government of Algeria. These States never missed an opportunity, at the United Nations or elsewhere, to denounce the neocolonialism of the Western powers, whom they accused of trying to "balkanize" the African continent. They demanded the immediate withdrawal of all foreign troops from African soil and characterized many of the African leaders who did not share their point of view as "puppets" of the West (Good 3–15).

The radicalism of the States in this group was probably best illustrated by the attitude they adopted toward the Algerian, Congolese, and Mauritanian crises at the United Nations. On the Algerian question, they demanded the immediate withdrawal of France and the holding of a referendum under the auspices of the UN in order to allow the Algerian people to exercise its right to self-determination and to decide on its own future. On the Congolese crisis, the Casablanca States demanded either the direct intervention of UN forces to restore the (left-wing) government of Prime Minister Patrice Lumumba or, in the alternative, the complete withdrawal of all UN troops from the Congo, thus allowing a completely inter-African military force to take control of the situation (Spencer 375–386; Kloman 387–404). With regard to Mauritania, a former French colony on the Moroccan border, the Casablanca Group maintained that it ought not to be an independent "puppet" State, but rather an integral part of the Kingdom of Morocco. Although, like many other French colonies, Mauritania gained its independence in November 1960, it did not immediately become a Member of the UN. The Casablanca States succeeded, with the help of the Soviet Union and the East Bloc countries, in blocking its admission to the UN until October 1961.

Even though these States did not have a formal or institutionalized structure, they all endorsed the *Casablanca Charter*, which laid down the fundamental principles underpinning the group. At the international level, they declared themselves non-aligned with respect to the two major ideological blocs; they emphasized non-interference by foreign States in the affairs of African countries; and they demanded an end to European colonialism in Africa. The *Casablanca Charter* also called for greater economic cooperation among African States and for the harmonization of their policies in order to facilitate the eventual unification of the continent. Additionally, the Casablanca States declared their support for all African nationalist movements seeking to unburden themselves from the yoke of European colonialism and neocolonialism.

Initially, it appeared as though this rhetoric would be matched by concrete action, as Ghana and Guinea, the first two Sub-Saharan African States to win their independence from European colonial powers, decided in 1958 to come together and form the Union of African States. This was quite remarkable, considering that the one was Anglophone and the other Francophone, and in December 1960, the newly independent Mali became the third Member of the Union. This new Union, cast in the monolithic mold of the Soviet Union, was projected as the precursor to a single African State covering the entire continent (Marcum 3–18). The leaders stressed a high level of ideological conformity, militancy, and discipline, and attempted at every opportunity to export their revolutionary ideology into other African States.

Unfortunately, probably due to its radical ideology, the Casablanca Group did not win many converts among the newly independent African States. Its Members were accused of fomenting unrest in neighboring countries and of promoting a vision of a united Africa that would leave them as its leaders. In the end, like their archrivals in the Francophone camp, the Casablanca States agreed to dissolve their group and to join with all the others under the umbrella of the OAU in 1963.

Chapter Three

The Monrovia Group

In between these two extremes was the Monrovia Group, which included the more pragmatic or less ideologically committed African States such as Liberia, Ethiopia, Nigeria and other English-speaking countries. Its constitutive conference, which took place in the Liberian capital, Monrovia, from May 8–12, 1961, was until then the single largest gathering of African leaders, bringing together 15 Heads of State and Government, as well as five other ministerial delegations. Interestingly, some Member States of the Brazzaville Group attended the conference while none of the Casablanca States did. It thus appeared as if the fundamental political cleavage on the African continent was between the Casablanca Group on the one hand and the rest of independent Africa on the other.

Perhaps the most important outcome of the Monrovia Conference was the adoption of Monrovia Doctrine, which defined a framework for international relations among African States. The principal components of that doctrine included respect for the sovereignty and territorial integrity of all African States; non-interference in the internal affairs of other States; the peaceful resolution of international conflicts; and harmonious diversity and tolerance for the differences between various African States and peoples. The participating States also announced their intention to intensify their level of cooperation in the fields of trade, commerce, culture, education, transportation, and communications (Marcum 5).

On the Congolese crisis, the Monrovia Doctrine reaffirmed the Member States' support for the UN's activities, while on the Algerian question it requested France and other colonial powers to grant independence to the African territories under their control. The Nigerian Prime Minister, Sir Abubakar Tafawa Balewa, emerged as the dominant figure at that conference, largely as a

result of his appeal for moderation and pragmatism with regard to both continental integration and relations with the outside world.

The Monrovia Group held another conference in Lagos, Nigeria, from January 25–30, 1962. Once again, 20 independent African States participated,
with 17 of them represented by their Heads of State or Government, thus
breaking the African record established the previous year in the Liberian capital. One significant difference this time around, however, was the fact that
Libya and Tunisia had decided to boycott the conference in protest over the
failure to invite the Provisional Government of Algeria. While the void created by their absence was quickly filled by the participation of (Belgian)
Congo and Tanganyika, the incident revealed another critical dimension to
African politics and underscored one more line of cleavage: the North-South
divide. In essence, with Morocco, the United Arab Republic (Egypt), and the
Sudan also refusing to participate in the activities of the Monrovia Group,
there seemed to be a clear split between Arab States of North Africa and the
Black States of Sub-Saharan Africa. Did the Sahara desert constitute an ob-
stacle to African unity? This was a question that the African leaders were
forced to answer in the short term (Endeley 154).

Meanwhile, the participants at the Lagos Conference examined various
proposals aimed at creating a continental organization. In particular, they discussed a draft charter presented by Liberia as well as the possibility of expanding the Organization of African and Malagasy Economic Cooperation
(the Brazzaville Group's OAMCE) to include non-Francophone States. They
also adopted a resolution calling for an amendment of the Charter of the
United Nations to allow for a greater representation of the African continent
within the various UN organs, especially the Security Council and the Economic and Social Council (ECOSOC) (Sterne 3–23). Later, on December 20,
1962, some 16 Member States of this group signed the *Lagos Charter* establishing a new and enlarged Organization of African and Malagasy Cooperation (also better known by its French acronym OCAM).

If the States of the Casablanca Group could be described as "radicals" and
those in the Brazzaville Group as "conservatives," then those in the Monrovia
Group must have been the "moderates." In terms of ideology, for instance, the
Member States of this group displayed a certain level of neutrality with respect to the two opposing blocs engaged in the Cold War without denying
themselves the benefits of maintaining relations with either camp. Their political rhetoric was often devoid of the emotional content that characterized
the pronouncements of the Casablanca Group, and they often preferred to fo-
cus on institutions rather than on personalities or on symbolism. Moreover,
despite including some of the UAM's Francophone States, the Monrovia
Group tended to be pragmatic rather than dogmatic. It perceived neither the

capitalist system of the West nor the communist system of the East as Africa's enemy. In its view, the real problems for the African leaders to tackle were those of development and cooperation. To that end, the group was willing to deal with all the States of the world regardless of ideology (Good 6).

Here again, the Congolese crisis would appear to be an excellent basis for comparison to the extent that it brought out the different groups' attitudes towards the UN. Thus, unlike the Casablanca Group that called for the immediate withdrawal of UN troops, the Monrovia Group consistently supported the UN's activities to restore the legitimate government and the rule of law in the Congo. Some of the Monrovia Group States even provided troops to the international peace-keeping force deployed in the Congo, while others pushed for a strengthening of the UN's mandate to enable it intervene more effectively and maintain the Congo's territorial integrity (Andemicael 10; Nyangoni 37; Hoffman 331–361). However, the Monrovia Group carefully rejected any calls for the UN to take direct and complete control of the Congo.

Finally, since the Brazzaville Group was, to a certain extent, a sub-set of this group, and in order to avoid duplicity at the international level, following the creation of OCAM in Lagos in 1962, the Monrovia Group decided to adopt the Brazzaville Group's institutions and to use its Permanent Secretariat at the UN Headquarters in New York to coordinate its diplomatic activities. After the creation of the Organization of African Unity a few months later, and after some three years of ideological rivalry and personality conflicts, all the independent African States (except South Africa) agreed to come together to create a single African Group in order to better present and defend their continent's interests before the international community in general and at the UN in particular.

Chapter Four

Toward a Single African Group

With three competing blocs of independent States spread out across Africa, the feat of achieving continental unity appeared quite daunting in the early 1960s. On the surface, it seemed as if it would be impossible for the African leaders to put aside their ideological differences or personality conflicts and come together in the interest of African unity. In the end, it took the personal prestige and pragmatism of Emperor Haile Selassie of Ethiopia to bring all the African leaders together in his capital city, Addis Ababa, in May of 1963 for the All-African Conference. After a lot of negotiation and compromise, a final agreement was reached on the establishment of a new umbrella organization that would subsume the erstwhile competing blocs. Thus was born the Organization of African Unity (OAU).

However, the Addis Ababa conference did not end just with the creation of the OAU and the adoption of its *Charter*. The leaders also held extensive discussions on such important issues as Pan-Africanism, decolonization, *apartheid*, economic development, and international relations. At the end of the conference they adopted six separate resolutions, of which the third, captioned "Africa, Non-Alignment and the United Nations," bore directly on the organization of their continental caucusing group at the UN. The resolution invited the governments of the various African States, without prejudice to their membership in the Afro-Asian Group, to instruct their Permanent Representatives at the United Nations to establish an African Group in order to increase cooperation among them and to better coordinate their strategies on matters of common concern. This, then, is the legal basis for the creation of the African Group at the UN. The three sub-groups had finally agreed to put aside their differences and to work together under a single umbrella caucusing group.

Chapter Five

Caucusing Groups in General

Although the Charter of the United Nations does not specifically refer to regional blocs or caucusing groups, it is common practice for Member States from the same part of the world or sharing the same political ideology to set up caucusing groups for the purpose of formulating a common position on key issues (Bailey 1989; Hovet 1960). This practice was developed pursuant to Article 23, Paragraph 1 of the Charter, which recommends that there be an equitable geographical distribution of seats within the various organs of the Organization in order to ensure some measure of representation for all of the world's peoples. It is on the basis of this provision, for instance, that the non-permanent seats on the Security Council are allocated. As a consequence there are currently five officially recognized regional groups at the UN. They are: the African Group, the Asian Group, the Latin America and Caribbean Group, the Eastern European Group, and the Western European and Others Group.

The African Group at the United Nations today includes all 52 independent States that used to be Members of the now-defunct Organization of African Unity (OAU) and are currently Members of the new African Union (AU), plus Morocco, which, while remaining a Member of the UN, withdrew from the OAU in 1985 and has so far not joined the AU. (See Table 5.1) This Group, comprising about 28 percent of the UN's membership, has the potential to be a significant player on the international political scene and for that reason alone, deserves considerable analytical scrutiny. Yet, its structure and functioning seldom have been the object of any major scientific study. It is hoped that the analysis presented in the next section will be a first step in the right direction.

Table 5.1. Composition of the African Group at the United Nations (May 2008)

State Name (Old Name)	Independence Date	Admission to UN
Algeria	July 3, 1962	October 8, 1962
Angola	November 11, 1976	December 1, 1976
Benin (Dahomey)	August 1, 1960	September 20, 1960
Botswana	September 30, 1966	October 17, 1966
Burkina Faso (Upper Volta)	August 5, 1960	September 20, 1960
Burundi	June 30, 1962	September 18, 1962
Cameroon	January 1, 1960	September 20, 1960
Cape Verde	July 5, 1975	September 16, 1975
Central African Republic	August 13, 1960	September 20, 1960
Chad	August 11, 1960	September 20, 1960
Comoros	January 1, 1976	September 12, 1976
Congo-Brazzaville	August 15, 1960	September 20, 1960
Congo, Democratic Republic (Zaire)	June 30, 1960	September 20, 1960
Côte d'Ivoire	August 7, 1960	September 20, 1960
Djibouti	June 27, 1977	September 20, 1977
Egypt (United Arab Republic)	March 1, 1922	October 24, 1945*
Equatorial Guinea	October 12, 1968	November 12, 1968
Eritrea	May 24, 1993	May 28, 1993
Ethiopia		November 13, 1945*
Gabon	August 17, 1960	September 20, 1960
Gambia	February 18, 1965	September 21, 1965
Ghana (Gold Coast)	March 6, 1957	March 8, 1957
Guinea	October 2, 1958	December 12, 1958
Guinea-Bissau	September 24, 1973	September 17, 1974
Kenya	December 12, 1963	December 16, 1963
Lesotho	October 4, 1966	October 17, 1966
Liberia	July 26, 1847	November 2, 1945*
Libya	December 24, 1951	December 14, 1955

Madagascar (Malagasy)	June 26, 1960	September 20, 1960
Malawi	July 6, 1964	December 1, 1964
Mali	September 22, 1960	September 28, 1960
Mauritania	November 28, 1960	October 27, 1961
Mauritius	March 12, 1968	April 24, 1968
Morocco	March 2, 1956	November 12, 1956
Mozambique	June 25, 1975	September 16, 1975
Namibia (South West Africa)	March 21, 1990	April 23, 1990
Niger	August 3, 1960	September 20, 1960
Nigeria	October 1, 1960	October 7, 1960
Rwanda	July 1, 1962	September 18, 1962
Sao Tome and Principe	July 12, 1975	September 16, 1975
Senegal	August 20, 1960	September 28, 1960
Seychelles	June 29, 1976	September 21, 1976
Sierra Leone	April 27, 1961	September 27, 1961
Somalia	July 1, 1960	September 20, 1960
South Africa	May 31, 1910	November 7, 1945*
Sudan	January 1, 1956	November 12, 1956
Swaziland	September 6, 1968	September 24, 1968
Tanzania (Tanganyika & Zanzibar)	December 9, 1961	December 14, 1961
Togo	April 27, 1960	September 20, 1960
Tunisia	March 20, 1956	November 12, 1956
Uganda	October 9, 1962	October 25, 1962
Zambia	October 24, 1964	December 1, 1964
Zimbabwe (Rhodesia)	April 18, 1980	August 25, 1980

Legend: * = Founding Member of UN
Source: Endeley 23.

Part Two

The Structure and Functioning of the African Group

INTRODUCTION

Any analysis of the behavior of the African States at the UN must include a good understanding of the structure and functioning of the African Group. This is necessary in order to highlight its distinguishing traits and to illustrate the ways in which it differs from the other regional or ideological groups, such as the Afro-Asian Group or the Non-Aligned Movement (NAM), of which it is still a subset. However, this already difficult task is rendered more complicated by the lack of basic documents through which a researcher might be able to grasp at least a part of the reality underlying African diplomacy at the UN. This shortcoming notwithstanding, it is possible, through careful direct observation, to paint a fairly detailed and accurate picture of the functioning of the African Group at the UN and indeed within the broader international system. The data presented here has been derived mainly through such direct observation and participation in the work of the African Group, particularly during the 49th Session of the UN General Assembly. The analysis is also based in part on the consultation of the *Minutes of Meetings* and other *unpublished internal documents* of the African Group, as well as on informal interviews and discussions with African diplomats at the UN Headquarters in New York.

Following the establishment of the OAU in May 1963, the African Group at the UN was formally constituted in September of the same year at the opening of the 17th Session of the UN General Assembly. The office of the Executive Secretariat of the OAU at the UN was opened on December 1, 1963, and various other organs were set up in the course of the next several years as the need for them arose. The nine main organs of the African Group at the UN as of May 2003 are as follows:

I   The African Group of the Whole (Plenary Assembly)
II   The Chairman of the African Group
III   The Executive Committee
IV   The Executive Secretariat
V   The Committee on Candidatures
VI   The Expert Group on Economic Matters
VII   The Regional Coordinators
VIII   The Welcome Committee
IX   *Ad hoc* committees

The African Group of the Whole, under the direction of the Chairman of the African Group, is at the apex of the hierarchy and all the other organs report to it. The Executive Secretariat and Executive Committee are at the second tier of organs, followed at the next level by the Committee on Candidatures and the Expert Group on Economic Matters. Finally, the Regional Coordinators, the Welcome Committee, and various *Ad hoc* committees are located at the bottom of the ladder. (See Figure 1) While this is not an official classification of the organs, it seems to accurately reflect the functioning of the Group as observed, and this perception is shared by a number of international civil servants and diplomats in New York. The relative importance of the various organs is also apparent through the level of importance attached to them by the Secretariat as well as by the relative weight of their decisions and recommendations (Endeley 38).

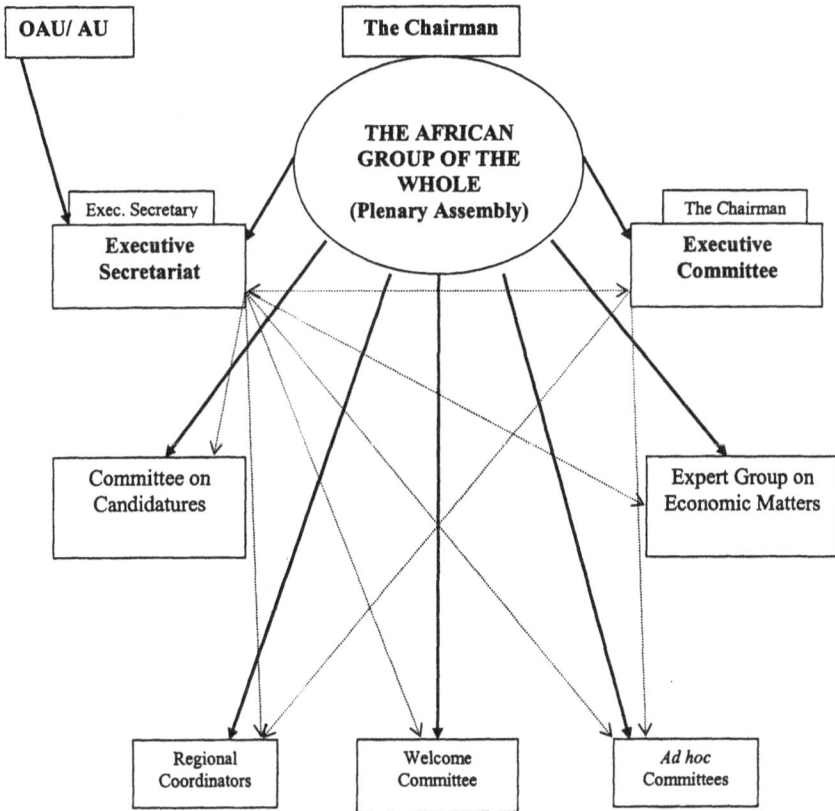

Figure 1.   Organizational Chart of the African Group at the UN (2003).
Source: Endeley 167.

Chapter Six

The African Group of the Whole

The African Group is comprised of all 53 independent African States that are Members of the UN as of May 2008 (see Table 5.1). All African States admitted to the UN have the right to belong to this group and to participate in its activities. However, its composition has not always been quite identical to that of the old OAU or the new AU. For example, Morocco, which withdrew in 1985 from the OAU over the latter's admission of the POLISARIO Front as the legitimate representative of Western Sahara, has remained an active Member of the African Group while South Africa, which was deliberately excluded from the Group from 1963 to 1994 due to its *apartheid* policies and its illegal occupation of Namibian territory, is now a very influential Member of the Group.

The main purpose of the African Group is to harmonize and coordinate the diplomatic strategies of the African States within the framework of the UN. Through a series of very regular formal and informal meetings, the representatives of the different African States share their views on all the issues before any of the various UN organs and agencies at any given time. This often results in them formulating a common African position aimed at solving specific problems. A cursory glance at the weekly meeting schedules of the various regional and caucusing groups represented at the UN Headquarters in New York would seem to indicate that the African Group probably meets as frequently as any other, especially in the period around the opening of the General Assembly sessions in the autumn of each year.

The African Group of the Whole, or plenary assembly, is the highest organ of the African Group at the UN. It is composed of the Permanent Representatives to the UN of all 53 African States, or other competent and duly accredited personnel, usually with the rank of ambassador. This is the only organ empowered to take decisions on behalf of the Group and all the other organs are answerable to it. Not all Member States attend all meetings, but discussions generally proceed on schedule regardless of the number of States present. However, in order for any decisions to be taken, a quorum of at least half the membership (27 States) must be attained. The plenary assembly meets in ordinary session at least twice a month, usually on the second and fourth Thursdays, in order to discuss issues on the UN agenda and to exchange views on matters of importance to the African continent. However, it can meet in extraordinary session at any time if so requested by its Chairman. In principle, any African State can ask the Chairman to call an extraordinary meeting of the Group, provided it can get assurances from at least half the number of Member States that they will attend, in order to attain a quorum.

The field of competence of the plenary assembly is quite vast, covering everything from the UN system to African international relations generally. Although it lacks the legal and financial means to enforce its decisions, the Group regularly issues recommendations on a wide range of subjects, the bulk of which concern the interests of the African continent within the UN framework. The Group has no written rules or regulations and it has developed its current practices and procedures essentially in an *ad hoc* manner over the years. However, the Permanent Representative of the African Union at the UN Headquarters in New York is required to keep the Secretary-General of the AU constantly informed of the Group's activities. The Secretary-General then uses his discretion in deciding whether or not to bring any specific issue to the attention of the AU's Executive Council.

The meetings of the African Group of the Whole and of all the other organs generally take place in the mid-sized conference rooms at the UN Headquarters in New York, such as the ECOSOC or the Trusteeship Council conference rooms. However, whenever there is no conference room available at the UN Headquarters, or when the Group wishes to discuss an issue it considers sensitive or would like to keep confidential, it meets in the Office of the Permanent Observer for the AU, located a short distance from the UN Headquarters. The meetings are conducted in English or in French, with simultaneous interpretation between the two languages provided by either the UN or the AU, depending on the venue of the meeting. The seating arrangement for this body and all organs of the African Group is according to the alphabetical order of their name in English, with the appropriate name plaque in front of the Permanent Representative of each Member State. During the sessions the Representatives refer to one another by their formal title (e.g., "The Honorable Representative from Cameroon") rather than by name. The meetings are always conducted under the leadership of the Chairman of the African Group, who is necessarily the Permanent Representative of one of the African States or his deputy. (The selection of the Chairman of the African Group is discussed below.)

The agenda for each meeting of the African Group of the Whole is set in advance by the Executive Secretariat of the AU in collaboration with the Chairman of the Group. Drawn up in English and French and distributed to participating Ambassadors at the start of each meeting, it often reflects the main issues before the UN General Assembly or Security Council, or questions under the active consideration of the AU's Executive Council. Sometimes, however, the agenda is dictated by the unfolding of events on the African political scene. On some occasions, the Group may meet not to undertake normal discussions, but for a special event. Possible reasons for such a special session be to hear a special report or to be briefed by an African international civil servant; to hear special presentations from very important personalities, such as African cabinet ministers visiting New York; to be addressed by the Administrators of various UN programs and agencies who may want to inform the Group of their agencies' activities on the continent; or even to receive the Representatives of different regional caucusing groups that wish to secure the support of the African States on a particular matter.

The African Group of the Whole also meets to consider the suggestions and recommendations of its own subsidiary organs. For instance, it is ultimately responsible for selecting the candidates to take up the seats reserved for the African continent on the various UN organs, for which it relies quite heavily on the recommendations of the Committee on Candidatures. In reality, any State, African or other, that wishes to occupy a seat on any of the UN organs or agencies quickly realizes the importance of winning the endorsement of the African Group, especially if such a State hopes to be elected by the UN General Assembly, where the African States account for more than one-quarter of the total number of votes.

The African Group makes its decisions and recommendations not on the basis of a formal vote, but rather through an explicit consensus reached at the end of a long discussion, often quite similar to an African *palaver*. Consequently, the decision-making process can sometimes be tedious and drawn out, since even the most controversial questions must be debated at length and until the Members arrive at a decision. The tendency of certain African Representatives to be long-winded also adds to the length of the meetings. In the past, the ideological cleavage of the bipolar Cold War era further contributed to the tedium of these Group meetings, as the supporters of each camp tried hard to prevail over their opponents. However, the impassioned debates continue even today, and it is not unusual for the UN's exasperated interpreters to signal their intention to stop working right in the middle of one of the Group's meetings!

While the African Group of the Whole is the only organ with the authority to take decisions or issue directives, its decisions are not legally binding on the Member States and cannot be enforced. In the end the individual States reserve the right to exercise their independence and sovereignty. As a matter of fact, it is quite commonplace to see Member States acting contrary to the recommendations of the Group. With regard to candidatures for the most coveted posts on UN bodies, for instance, when the plenary assembly endorses one Member State's application, another Member State that is dissatisfied with the selection may choose to present its own candidate to run against the so-called African candidate during elections in the General Assembly.

This was precisely what happened in 1977 during the Group's effort to select a candidate to occupy one of the seats reserved for the African continent on the UN Security Council. At that time, Nigeria, which had already served one term on the Council and wanted another, opposed the African Group's choice of Niger, which had not yet served on the Council. The official explanation for Nigeria's objection to the Group's choice was the fact that the OAU's Council of Ministers had never formally upheld the selection criteria used by the African Group's Committee on Candidatures. However, the officious reason for Nigeria's behavior was probably the fact that the military regime of General Obasanjo wanted to occupy the prestigious position one last time before handing over power to a civilian government. Nigeria therefore presented its candidature for the same seat and deployed all necessary tactics to ensure victory, including organizing extravagant parties and importing troupes of dancers from home to impress its guests. In the end, after six rounds of voting in the UN General Assembly, Nigeria won over the African Group's preferred candidate (Amate 200–202).

Chapter Seven

The Chairman of the African Group

The Chairman is the leader of the African Group and the official spokesman of African diplomacy at the UN. He is at the same time the symbol of African unity and the representative of Africa's peoples in their relations with the international community. He presides over all meetings of the African Group of the Whole and the Executive Committee, and is the only one authorized to call a meeting of those bodies. He also has the power to undertake negotiations or take decisions on the Group's behalf, and is answerable only to the plenary assembly. The Chairman works in close collaboration with the Executive Secretariat of the AU in New York as well as with the Executive Committee to set the agenda for meetings of the African Group of the Whole. However, in case of an emergency, any Member State can request the Chairman to call an extraordinary meeting of the Group, provided it has the support of a sufficient number of States (at least 27) to constitute a quorum. Although the Chairman has the authority to take certain decisions or to undertake certain actions on his own initiative, especially when it is not possible to obtain the approval of the plenary assembly, the usual practice is that he consults with the Members of the Executive Committee before embarking on any major course of action.

The Chairmanship of the Group rotates on a monthly basis, by the alphabetical order of the States' names in English. This little detail is of critical importance particularly with respect to those States whose names are not written in the same way in English and French and/or the other official languages of the UN. Chad, for instance, comes right after the Central African Republic rather than after Tanzania, since its name is written in English without the "T" in French (Tchad). The same is true of Equatorial Guinea, whose name starts with the letter "E" in English but with a "G" in Spanish, its official language.

Equatorial Guinea follows immediately after Egypt, rather than after Guinea-Bissau.

This practice of rotation was instituted at the inception of the African Group in 1963 both in order to give each Member State the opportunity to have its turn at the helm of the Group and to prevent some of the more ambitious delegates from assuming a permanent leadership role. Here, once again, there appears to be a direct link between the practice of African diplomacy at the UN and the prevailing context of ideological rivalry of the Cold War era. By frequently rotating the leadership position, the Group has successfully avoided being dominated by one ideological camp or the other. The practice also allows for a certain degree of predictability in the Group's affairs and allows the Member States to plan their activities long before assuming the Chair.

To cite a concrete example, at the opening of the 49th Session of the UN General Assembly in September 1994, the Chairman of the African Group was the Permanent Representative of Gabon, followed in October by his counterpart from The Gambia, in November by the Ghanaian Representative, and in December by the Representative of Guinea. Considering that the African Group currently has 53 Members, each of them can expect to assume the chairmanship approximately once every four-and-a-half years! It should therefore come as no surprise that each State eagerly awaits its turn to be the mouthpiece of the African continent at the UN.

However, the States are not obliged to accept the responsibility of serving as Chairman if their turn comes at an inopportune moment. In January 1995, for example, the Permanent Representative of Guinea-Bissau indicated that his government was unable at that time to succeed Guinea and assume the leadership of the Group. Among the reasons cited was the fact that his State was then already chairing the Committee on Candidatures, which involved a lot of work, and which automatically made the Guinea-Bissau Representative a member of the Executive Committee, as well as the fact that Guinea-Bissau's Permanent Mission at the UN lacked sufficient personnel to perform all the tasks assigned to it. That country therefore forfeited its turn to the next State on the list, Kenya.

Member States are not allowed to trade turns with each other. They are expected to either accept the responsibility immediately or forfeit their turn and wait another four years or so. In another example, when Liberia was unable to succeed Lesotho in March 1995, the Permanent Representative of Libya became the Chairman for that month. In that case, according to one Liberian diplomat, the civil war ravaging his country at the time forced the State to control its spending and to reduce the size of its diplomatic staff at the UN. These two examples illustrate, among other things, that being Chairman of the African Group entails certain financial costs as well as a significant investment in terms of the time and energy spent in diplomatic negotiations and discussions on the Group's behalf.

The Chairman also represents the African Group at the monthly meetings between the Secretary General of the UN and the Chairs of the five regional groups. Additionally, he presides over all events and ceremonies, both formal and informal, organized by the Group. These often include cultural events, dinner parties in honor of new or departing African ambassadors, or the celebration of Africa Day, the anniversary of the founding of the OAU, on May 25th of each year.

While one disadvantage of the frequent rotation at the Group's helm seems to be a lack of continuity, this problem is partially resolved by including the immediate past Chairman as well as the next one in line in the Executive Committee. Furthermore, at the end of his term, each outgoing Chairman is expected to fully brief his successor on all unresolved issues as well as on the major items on the Group's agenda for the coming month. On the first convenient business day of each month, the AU's Permanent Observer at the UN (or Executive Secretary, as explained below) organizes a short meeting between the outgoing and incoming Chairmen in order to facilitate the transition and the transfer of files. This gives the new leader a fair idea of what he must accomplish during the coming month.

Finally, it should be noted that the Chairman of the African Group at the UN is primarily a symbol of African unity and the official mouthpiece of the African continent in its relations with the outside world, at least within the framework of the UN. His main asset seems to be the prestige of his position, backed as it is by the numerical strength of the African Group. However, the Chairman is not a sovereign authority and is ultimately responsible to the African Group of the Whole, or plenary assembly, where all Member States are represented.

Chapter Eight

The Executive Committee

The Executive Committee is relatively small and fairly representative of all the regions and States of the African continent. It is one of the key organs of the African Group and its primary responsibility is to implement the decisions and to coordinate the diplomatic strategies of the African Group of the Whole. In certain emergency situations, it can also take decisions or actions in the Group's name, particularly if the Chairman is unable or unwilling to act unilaterally. The Chairman of the African Group is also the Chairman of the Executive Committee and has the sole authority to call its meetings. However, just as in the case of the plenary assembly, he usually works in close collaboration with the Office of the Permanent Observer for the AU in New York. Moreover, the agenda for the Executive Committee's meetings usually reflects the main preoccupations of the African Group of the Whole, which often leaves to the Committee the treatment of the most sensitive questions or of matters requiring speedy action.

The Executive Committee is required by its own established practice to meet at least once each month or twelve times a year. Its meetings usually take place on the first Tuesday of each month, in part to avoid having a scheduling conflict with the African Group of the Whole, which meets on the second and fourth Thursdays. In practice, however, the Executive Committee meets as frequently as necessary to accomplish its duties, particularly when the Chairman is in need of counsel or when there is an issue of particular importance to the African continent on the agenda of one of the main UN bodies, such as the Security Council or the General Assembly. The Executive Committee is comprised of the following twelve persons:

1. The current Chairman of the African Group
2. The immediate past Chairman of the African Group

3. The immediate next Chairman of the African Group
4. The Permanent Representative of the State of the current Chairman of the AU
5. The Permanent Representative of the State of the immediate past Chairman of the AU
6. The Regional Coordinator for the Central Africa region
7. The Regional Coordinator for the East Africa region
8. The Regional Coordinator for the North Africa region
9. The Regional Coordinator for the Southern Africa region
10. The Regional Coordinator for the West Africa region
11. The Chairman of the Committee on Candidatures
12. The Permanent Observer for the AU to the UN

The composition of the Executive Committee has a lot of political undertones. The first and most obvious one is the AU's desire to exercise a certain measure of control over the activities of the African Group, particularly the decision-making process. Thus, not only is the continental organization's Permanent Observer at the UN a member of the Executive Committee, but so too are the Permanent Representatives from the States of the current and immediate past Chairmen of the AU. This, coupled with the fact that the Permanent Observer is required to report to the Secretary-General of the AU on all the meetings and activities of the Executive Committee, surely creates a direct line of communication between New York and Addis Ababa.

Secondly, the Executive Committee is also designed to ensure a high level of continuity in the activities and functioning of the African Group. Even though its composition always changes slightly from one month to the next, there is usually a sufficient number of other elements left to guarantee that continuity. For instance, every Chairman of the Group remains a member of the Executive Committee for at least three months: one month each as the immediate next, current, and immediate past Chairman. For the Permanent Representative of the State of the Chairman of the AU, however, the duration within the Executive Committee is much greater. Since the term of the AU Chairman is for one year and not immediately renewable, his Representative can expect to stay on the Committee for up to two years (as the Representative of the current and then of the immediate past Chairman). As for the AU's Permanent Observer for the UN, he stays permanently on the Committee. Incidentally, the Permanent Observers for the OAU and now for the AU have tended to stay in New York for more than five years at a time, making them a permanent fixture within the Executive Committee. The result has been that the OAU and AU have wielded considerable influence, even control, over the activities of the African Group at the UN, since it is in effect the Executive

Committee that formulates and articulates many of the decisions taken by the African Group of the Whole.

A third important aspect of the composition of the Executive Committee is the desire to have a measure of regional balance so that no single region ends up dominating the others. The presence of the Coordinators from each of the five regions of the continent ensures not only that the interests of the various geographical regions will be taken into consideration, but also that each of them plays an active role in the overall decision-making process. It should be noted, however, that the length of their mandates differs from one region to the next, and obviously this can have an impact on the composition of the Executive Committee.

Finally, whenever a question of great importance to the African continent is on the agenda of one of the main UN organs, such as the Security Council or ECOSOC, the African States occupying a seat on those organs are invited to participate in the deliberations of the Executive Committee. This was the case in early 1995, for instance, when the Security Council was holding preliminary discussions about the future of the United Nations Angola Verification Mission (UNAVEM). The three African Members of the Security Council at the time, Botswana, Nigeria, and Rwanda, were invited to participate in the meetings conducted in February 1995, during which the Executive Committee received a delegation from the OAU's Council of Ministers and prepared a plan of action for the subsequent UNAVEM debate at the Security Council.

Chapter Nine

The Executive Secretariat

The Executive Secretariat is arguably the most important organ of the African Group at the UN. It is probably not an exaggeration to suggest that the African Group would be incapable of functioning properly in the absence of the Executive Secretariat. Yet, the very status of the Secretariat easily leads to confusion and needs to be clarified at the onset. It is apparent that this organ performs at least two distinct roles at the same time.

On the one hand, the office space occupied by the Executive Secretariat also hosts the official representation of the AU at the UN Headquarters in New York. In this capacity it bears the official title of Office of the Permanent Observer for the African Union to the United Nations, and this is the title that appears on its letterhead and official documents. (Prior to July 2002, it was known as the Permanent Observer Mission of the Organization of African Unity to the United Nations.) The significance of having the status of an Observer is that the AU is admitted to participate in most of the UN's activities, but it does not have a vote in the decision-making process. Another important factor here is that the head of this diplomatic mission bears the official title of Permanent Observer and has the rank of an Ambassador. The personnel working at the diplomatic mission are therefore international civil servants employed by the continental organization. Other regional organizations, such as the European Union, the Arab League, or the Organization of American States, also have observer status at the UN.

On the other hand, this AU office functions as the Executive Secretariat of the African Group at the UN. In that connection, it performs all the usual duties of a secretariat, such as typing, filing, or preparing and distributing official documents to the various African delegations to the UN. It also coordinates the activities of all the other organs of the African Group, including drawing up the agenda for all meetings and keeping the minutes. These are some of the reasons why the Secretariat appears indispensable to the proper functioning of the African Group. In this second capacity, also, the head of the office bears the title of Executive Secretary of the African Group, a title he uses in all of his internal correspondence with the various organs and Member States of the Group. It is mostly in his dealings with the UN that he uses the formal title of Permanent Observer for the AU.

The Executive Secretariat is funded directly and exclusively by the AU from its Headquarters in Addis Ababa, Ethiopia. The funds needed to operate the Executive Secretariat and to pay the salaries of its personnel are drawn directly from the AU's regular annual budget, which in turn comes from the annual contributions of the Member States of the continental organization. In that regard, it seems neither unfair nor inaccurate to State that of all the Member States of the African Group at the UN, Morocco is the only one that does not contribute financially to the smooth functioning of the Executive Secretariat, having withdrawn from the continental organization in 1985. This state of affairs is not always appreciated and the hostility of certain African Representatives toward Morocco is often only thinly veiled and entails certain diplomatic and social costs to that State. For example, Morocco often finds itself left out when meetings of the African Group are conducted in the AU's premises. Similarly, whenever a delegation from the AU Council of Ministers is visiting New York to meet with the African Representatives, Morocco is usually not invited and therefore cannot participate in the decision-making process.

The Executive Secretary in New York is appointed by the AU's Executive Council upon the recommendation of the Secretary-General of the AU. Since the Executive Council also tends to function by consensus rather than by vote, each Member State of the African Group, through its Ministers of Foreign Affairs, has the opportunity to participate in the selection of the Executive Secretary. It would appear that the desired characteristics that the person holding this post must possess include: a lot of diplomatic and administrative experience, a good understanding of the UN system, mastery of both English and French and, of course, the support of a few key African States.

The Executive Secretary attends and participates directly in all meetings of the African Group of the Whole and is always seated on the podium next to the Chairman, which could serve as a measure of his importance within the Group. Since December 1st, 1963, when the office first opened its doors under the banner of the OAU, several different persons have held the post of Executive Secretary, and all of their portraits are prominently displayed in the offices of the Executive Secretariat. The last few persons to hold the post before the demise of the OAU in 2002 included two Malians, Messrs. Mamadou

Thiam and Dramane Ouattara (1974–1978), a Nigerian, Mr. Oumarou Yous-souffou (1978–1989), and two Senegalese, Messrs. Ibrahima Sy (1990–1997) and Ahmadou Kébé (1997–2002).

It seems apparent once again that even in the selection of the top diplomatic personnel, the erstwhile tensions of the colonial era continue to have an impact. In this case, the practice of alternating between Anglophone and Francophone nationals appears like one of the compromise measures that the Group adopted in order to maintain the unity it achieved after the merger of the three competing groups in 1963. It is interesting to note that the Portuguese- and Arabic-speaking African States did not manage to challenge the dominance of the two other linguistic groups.

For much of the period leading up to the dissolution of the OAU in 2002, the staff at the Executive Secretariat in New York was typically comprised of some 20 personnel from various African States. There are indications that this practice is being continued under the new AU. The 20 staff members could be divided into two broad categories loosely termed professional personnel (usually about 14 persons) and general service personnel (about 6 persons). Only the professionals were recruited directly by the OAU in Addis Ababa and are considered diplomatic personnel, the others being hired locally in New York. However, they all have to be nationals of African States, and an effort is always made to ensure an equitable representation of the various geographical and linguistic interests on the continent. These personnel are further spread out among six separate sections within the Executive Secretariat, depending on the specific tasks performed. The functioning of the entire office is under the direct supervision of the Executive Secretary, who is answerable directly to the AU, and perhaps indirectly to the African Group at the UN.

The first section is the private office of the Executive Secretary, where all the major decisions concerning the operation of the Executive Secretariat are taken. All of the important correspondence related to the African Group goes through this office before being redirected to any other section for appropriate action. It is the Executive Secretary who, in collaboration with the Chairman, draws up the agenda for the African Group of the Whole and the Executive Committee. He also presides over a fortnightly meeting with other top personnel at the Executive Secretariat, usually on the first and third Mondays of the month, during which the main issues affecting the operation of the Executive Secretariat are discussed. He has a Private Secretary to assist him in the execution of his duties, and in his absence the Assistant Executive Secretary runs the office on an interim basis.

The second component of the Executive Secretariat is the Political Affairs Section, which is arguably the one most directly involved with the activities of the African Group at the UN and its principal organs. It is made up of two or three professionals, each of whom typically has an advanced degree and some political experience at the national or international level. The Political Affairs Section also has a secretary to assist with its operations. At least one representative of this section attends all of the meetings of any organ of the African Group and is responsible for drawing up the minutes as well as for providing the Representatives of the Member States with supplementary information if the need arises. One of the key functions of the Political Affairs Section, as described below, is to work with the Committee on Candidatures to establish the criteria for selecting African candidates to occupy the highly coveted posts and seats on the main UN bodies, such as the Security Council or the Bureau of the General Assembly.

The Economic Affairs Section is relatively less active and is primarily responsible for coordinating the activities of the Expert Group of Economic Matters, an organ of the African Group. It is usually comprised of two professional economists and a secretary, and is responsible for monitoring the agenda and activities of United Nations Economic and Social Council (ECOSOC) and the various UN programs and agencies working in the field of economic development.

The Administrative Affairs Section is quite small, consisting of just one professional with a background in accounting and book-keeping, and a secretary. It is responsible for managing the Secretariat's budget and for channeling the employees' salaries from the AU's Headquarters in Addis Ababa to their respective bank accounts in New York and elsewhere. It controls all of the Secretariat's expenses, from travel allowances to entertainment for guests at receptions and printer cartridges for the office computers. It also is required to submit a monthly statement of the Executive Secretariat's expenditures back to Addis Ababa.

The Conference Services Section includes an Archivist who keeps the official records and documents of the Executive Secretariat and of the African Group, and two AU Translators/Interpreters, the one working from English to French and the other in the opposite direction. They assist in preparing documents that are distributed to the various African delegations in New York or forwarded to the AU in Ethiopia. They also provide simultaneous interpretation of speeches and discussions at meetings of various organs of the African Group, particularly when such meetings take place on the premises of the AU's Executive Secretariat in New York, but also if the meetings take place at the UN Headquarters and there are no UN interpreters available.

Finally, the General Services Section is made up of about six non-professional personnel who perform a multiplicity of tasks, including cleaning the offices, making coffee for staff and guests, or serving as chauffeur, courier or janitor. The people in this division are generally recruited locally in New York and have no real connection with the Headquarters in Addis Ababa other than the fact that they are citizens of AU Member States.

Chapter Ten

The Committee on Candidatures

As the name itself suggests, the primary purpose of the Committee on Candidatures is to process the applications of the Member States for the posts and seats reserved for the African continent on the various organs, agencies and programs of the UN system. The committee is responsible for examining all the applications submitted by the African States and for formulating recommendations addressed to the African Group of the Whole, or plenary assembly, which is the sole organ with the power to make decisions or to endorse African candidates. It is now a standard requirement that any African delegation in New York that wishes to hold a post or occupy a seat in one of the UN organs or programs must submit a written application to the Committee on Candidatures, via the Executive Secretariat of the AU at the UN Headquarters in New York.

This very powerful Committee is made up of the Permanent Representatives of only nine Member States selected on the basis of an equitable geographical representation of the five regions of the African continent, for a renewable two-year term. The mandate usually extends from January 1st of one year to December 31st of the following year. The Chairman of the Committee on Candidatures is selected by an explicit consensus among the nine Members and holds the post throughout the duration of their mandate. An Ambassador's personal abilities as a diplomat can be very useful, and the most experienced Representatives seem to have less difficulty persuading their counterparts to select them for this important post. The Chairman of the Committee on Candidatures is also automatically a Member of the Executive Committee of the African Group, thus making the position a very powerful one. The West African region, with 16 of the 53 Member States, has three of the nine seats on the Committee; the East Africa region, with 12 Member States, has two seats, while Central Africa, North Africa and Southern Africa have one each. The ninth seat usually alternates between the Central and Southern regions which, in this instance, would appear to be the most disadvantaged, as explained below (see Table 10.1).

The Committee on Candidatures does not have a fixed meeting schedule and can convene at any time as the need arises. However, its busiest periods are in late March and early April of every year. This is because the African Group of the Whole decided many years ago that the 31st of March of each year will be the deadline for Member States to submit their applications if they wish to occupy a seat on any UN body beginning at the next session of the General Assembly, which usually starts in the following September. The Committee needs a quorum of two-thirds (or six out of nine Members) in order to formulate and adopt recommendations to be presented to the African Group of the Whole. Although it can meet and hold general discussions with fewer participants, the tendency is not to meet at all unless a quorum is attained and concrete recommendations can be formulated.

The composition of the Committee on Candidatures has changed considerably in the post-Cold War and post-*apartheid* era, and the Southern African region appears to have been the main beneficiary of this change, having experienced a sharp increase in its relative weight in a very short time. This has been mainly due to the admission of Namibia to the UN and to the African Group in 1990, the admission of South Africa into the African Group in 1994, and the transfer of Angola from the Central to the Southern African region in 1995. With the independence of Eritrea in 1994, the East African region also saw a modest boost in its relative weight, while the Central African region appears to be the main loser (see Table 10.2).

Despite these changes, the composition of the Committee on Candidatures remains the subject of a heated debate within the African Group for two politically significant reasons. First, at the regional level, the Member States, through their Regional Coordinators, are constantly seeking to gain a relative advantage for their region with a view to increasing their chances of being selected to occupy the coveted seats. Secondly, at the State level, those Members currently serving on the Committee on Candidatures have a greater chance of promoting and defending their own candidature, or of promoting the candidate of their national government, for any position within the UN system. There are in fact many examples of African States which have managed, during their membership or chairmanship of the Committee on Candidatures, to get themselves elected to the UN Security Council.

Despite the principle of the sovereign equality of all Member States regardless of characteristics, the truth is that the smallest, poorest and weakest

Table 10.1. Geographical Distribution of the African States

I

WEST AFRICA (16 STATES)

1) Benin	2) Burkina Faso	3) Cape Verde
4) Côte d'Ivoire	5) Gambia	6) Ghana
7) Guinea	8) Guinea-Bissau	9) Liberia
10) Mali	11) Mauritania	12) Niger
13) Nigeria	14) Senegal	15) Sierra Leone
16) Togo		

II

EAST AFRICA (12 STATES)

1) Comoros	2) Djibouti	3) Eritrea
4) Ethiopia	5) Kenya	6) Madagascar
7) Mauritius	8) Seychelles	9) Somalia
10) Sudan	11) Tanzania	12) Uganda

III

CENTRAL AFRICA (10 STATES)

1) Burundi	2) Cameroon	3) Central African Republic
4) Chad	5) Congo-Brazzaville	6) Congo, Democratic Republic
7) Equatorial Guinea	8) Gabon	9) Rwanda
10) Sao Tome & Principe		

IV

SOUTHERN AFRICA (10 STATES)

1) Angola	2) Botswana	3) Lesotho
4) Malawi	5) Mozambique	6) Namibia
7) Swaziland	8) South Africa	9) Zambia
10) Zimbabwe		

V

NORTH AFRICA (5 STATES)

1) Algeria	2) Egypt	3) Libya
4) Morocco	5) Tunisia	

Source: Endeley 190.

Table 10.2. Weighting Table for the Geographical Distribution of Seats in the African Group

1.	West Africa	→ 16/53	= 30%
2.	East Africa	→ 12/53	= 23%
3.	Central Africa	→ 10/53	= 19%
4.	Southern Africa	→ 10/53	= 19%
5.	North Africa	→ 5/53	= 9%
	Total African Group	→ 53/53	= 100%

Number of Seats for Africa	West (16) 30%		East (12) 23%		Central (10) 19%		Southern (10) 19%		North (5) 9%		Float Seat
1	0.30		0.23		0.19		0.19		0.09		1
2	0.60		0.46		0.38		0.38		0.18		1
3	0.90	1	0.69	1	0.57		0.57		0.27		1
4	1.20	1	0.92	1	0.76		0.76		0.36		
5	1.50	1	1.15	1	0.95		0.95		0.45		
6	1.80	1	1.38	1	1.14	1	1.14	1	0.54	1	
7	2.10	2	1.61	2	1.33	1	1.33	1	0.63	1	
8	2.40	2	1.84	2	1.52	1	1.52	1	0.72	1	1
9	2.70	2	2.07	2	1.71	1	1.71	1	0.81	1	1
10	3.00	3	2.30	2	1.90	2	1.90	2	0.90	2	
11	3.30	3	2.53	3	2.09	2	2.09	2	0.99	2	
12	3.60	3	2.76	3	2.28	2	2.28	2	1.08	2	
13	3.90	3	2.99	3	2.47	2	2.47	2	1.17	3	1
14	4.20	4	3.22	3	2.66	3	2.66	3	1.26	3	
15	4.50	4	3.45	3	2.85	3	2.85	3	1.35	3	
16	4.80	5	3.68	3	3.04	3	3.04	3	1.44	3	
17	5.10	5	3.91	4	3.23	3	3.23	3	1.53	3	
18	5.40	5	4.14	4	3.42	3	3.42	3	1.62	3	1
19	5.70	6	4.37	4	3.61	3	3.61	3	1.71	3	1
20	6.00	6	4.60	4	3.80	4	3.80	4	1.80	4	2

Source: Permanent Observer Mission of the OAU to the UN (1998); Endeley 195.

ones always have to rely on the backing of the African Group, whereas the larger, richer and stronger ones can sometimes afford to dispense with the Group's endorsement and attempt to promote their candidates by themselves. A case in point is the 1977 incident involving Nigeria and Niger mentioned earlier. Furthermore, although all States wishing to serve on the Committee on Candidatures must meet the same rigid criteria set by the African Group, once selected they try to remain in place for as long as possible and to use this position as a stepping stone to other posts.

The Executive Secretariat of the OAU/AU is always represented at meetings of the Committee on Candidatures by one of the professional staff members at the Political Affairs Section, and sometimes by the Executive Secretary himself. On occasion, the Chairman of the African Group (or his representative) is invited to participate in the Committee's deliberations. Although the Committee does not have the power to make any decisions, its recommendations are usually adopted by the African Group of the Whole. This is perhaps an indication of the high level of confidence placed in the Committee's work and its rigorous application of the three objective criteria adopted by the Group for the evaluation of candidatures. These criteria are applied in all cases where there are more candidates than there are seats available.

The first criterion is the equitable geographical representation of all five regions of the African continent. Here, the Committee on Candidatures, working in collaboration with the Political Affairs Section of the Executive Secretariat, has established a mathematical weighting table for the allocation of seats according to the number of States in each region relative to the total number of Member States in the Group. According to the Committee's calculations, the relative weight (w) of each region is a function of the number of States in that region (n) relative to the total number of States in the African Group (N), expressed as a percentage.

This expression can be represented by the following equation:

$$w = n/N \times 100$$

Thus, the relative weight of the West African region, for example, would be $w = 16/53 \times 100 = 30\%$. This means that the West Africa region, which has 16 States, is entitled to thirty percent of the seats reserved for the African continent on any UN body. For example, in a situation where Africa is entitled to 18, the West Africa region would be able to claim five of those 18 seats ($30\% \times 18$). In situations where there are not enough seats to equitably represent all of the continent's regions, the Committee on Candidatures uses a system based on alternation between the disadvantaged regions. That is, a floating seat is shared between two or more regions that do not have equitable representation on the board, with each region holding the seat for a proportionate amount of the time.

The second criterion used by the Committee on Candidatures is the non-accumulation of posts by Member States of the African Group. In other words, the Representatives are discouraged from occupying several seats at the same time within the UN system. In situations where there is competition for the same seat, such as for the highly coveted African seats on the Security Council, the Economic and Social Council (ECOSOC), the Bureau of the General Assembly, or the governing bodies of specialized agencies like UNICEF or UNDP, priority is given to a State that does not already hold a seat in one of the other major bodies. However, this rule does not apply if there is only one candidate for the post.

Thirdly, the Committee on Candidatures tries to discourage Member States of the African Group from seeking reelection to consecutive mandates in the same position within any of the UN bodies. Thus, a State that has just completed a term on UNICEF's Executive Board, for instance, is generally requested not to immediately reapply for the same post. Whenever there are two or more candidates, the priority is always given to the State that is applying for the post for the first time. If all the competitors have already served on the body, then preference is given to candidate that has been away from the position for the longest time. Here, once again, the only exception is when there is only one candidate for the position.

Sometimes, when the negotiations are deadlocked, the Committee applies a fourth criterion known as the time factor. Under this rule of last resort, when two or more candidate States seem to be equally qualified to hold a seat, the Committee breaks the tie by looking at the date on which the Executive Secretariat received their respective applications. To that end, the African Group of the Whole had decided long ago that in order to be considered for positions that will be vacant during the next session of the UN General Assembly, which usually begins in September of each year, all candidatures must be submitted in writing to the Executive Secretariat no later than the preceding March 31st. Thus, as an example, any African State wishing to occupy a seat on any UN body during the 63rd Session of the General Assembly, which began in September 2008, should have submitted its application by March 31, 2008. Similarly, applications for the African seat on the Security Council that would become available on January 1, 2009, also had to be submitted no later than March 31, 2008.

By the same token, the Executive Secretariat is required to issue a duly stamped and dated official receipt for each application properly submitted. It has also adopted the practice of publishing at the end of each year, a catalogue of all African States holding seats or positions in all the different UN bodies. The catalogue, which is usually several dozen pages long, also contains a list of all the seats and positions that will become vacant during the following year as well as an indication of which States have already applied for what positions. The States therefore have about four months (December–March) to apply and negotiate among themselves.

This careful planning notwithstanding, the Committee on Candidatures often encounters a lot of difficulty in selecting the candidates to recommend to the African Group of the Whole. However, it is at the regional level that the real competition for the positions occurs. In that regard, the Regional Coordinators play a key role and can facilitate the work of the Committee by steering the negotiations within their respective regions to make a preliminary selection of the appropriate number of candidates based on the weighting table previously described. Ultimately, it is the African Group of the Whole that decides which States that will represent the African continent on any UN body. Even when the matter is submitted to a vote at the UN General Assembly, this is usually viewed as a mere formality.

Despite these clear rules of procedure, it has to be pointed out that the Committee on Candidatures occasionally deviates from the norm. In some circumstances, instead of applying the rules too rigidly, it can simply recommend to two competing States to negotiate with each other until one withdraws its candidature in favor of the other. This seems to be the preferred way of proceeding with regard to the African representation on the Security Council, and is perhaps the logical explanation for the presence of such rather small States as Djibouti, the Gambia, or Guinea-Bissau on that UN body in recent years.

This flexibility in the functioning of the Committee on Candidatures is also apparent when dealing with unusual occurrences. For instance, in the period leading up to the World Summit on Sustainable Development, which took place in Copenhagen, Denmark, from March 6–12, 1995, the Committee had to choose from among sixteen candidates to fill the seven Vice-Presidential positions reserved for the African continent on the Bureau of the Summit. Instead of strictly applying the standard criteria, however, the Committee based its recommendations primarily on two unusual factors. The first was whether the candidate-State had served on the Bureau of the two previous major UN conferences, namely the Children's Summit in New York in 1990, and Environmental Summit in Rio de Janeiro, Brazil, in 1992. The second factor was whether the Head of State or Government of the candidate-State would attend the Copenhagen Summit. Based on data furnished by the Executive Secretariat, the Committee on Candidatures finally recommended Burkina Faso and Guinea-Bissau from West Africa, Ethiopia and Sudan from the East, Cameroon from Central Africa, Zimbabwe from the Southern region, and Algeria from the North. This illustrates the willingness and ability of the Committee on Candidatures in particular and of the African Group in general to adapt to changing circumstances and to take account of new realities.

Chapter Eleven

The Expert Group
on Economic Matters

The Expert Group on Economic Matters is responsible for following developments on economic and social matters within the UN system that are likely to be of importance to the African continent. In particular, the Expert Group monitors very closely the activities of the Economic and Social Council (ECOSOC) and the various specialized agencies and subsidiary programs focusing on matters of economic and social development and welfare, such as UNDP, UNEP, UNHCR, or UNICEF. The African Group at the UN, through this organ, participates either directly or indirectly in the work of these bodies and attempts to defend the economic and social interests of the African people at every opportunity. The Expert Group also works in close collaboration with many non-governmental organizations (NGOs) undertaking various projects in Africa, including such prominent ones as the International Committee of the Red Cross, Doctors Without Borders, Oxfam, or CARE. It is often at the leading edge in formulating a common African position on economic and social questions and usually takes into consideration the specific demands of the different Member States of the African Group.

Despite its title, this Group is not necessarily comprised of professional economists. Rather, it is made up of the personnel at the various Permanent Missions of the African States in New York who are responsible for economic and social issues at the UN on behalf of their respective governments. These persons are usually called "Economic Experts," or "Experts" for short, even if they have no real expertise in economic matters. Like most of the other organs of the African Group, this Expert Group does not have the power to take any decisions. It can only issue recommendations, which the African Group of the Whole may accept or reject. The Economic Affairs Section at the Executive Secretariat is responsible for coordinating the activities of the Expert Group.

The Group also works in close collaboration with the various economic and social organs of the AU, as well as with the United Nations Economic Commission for Africa (ECA), which also has its Headquarters in Addis Ababa, Ethiopia.

The Expert Group meets at least once a month, usually on the third Thursday, but its meetings can be more frequent if necessary. The meetings are chaired by the designated Expert from the State of the Chairman of the African Group. That is, the Chairmen of the African Group and the Chairman of the Expert Group on Economic Matters are always from the same State and their mandates are for the same month. All Member States of the African Group are always represented at meetings of the Expert Group and here too, the seating is always arranged by the alphabetical order of their name in English.

While its agenda is general predictable and regular, there are periods when the Expert Group has a lot of different activities on its schedule. For instance, in the periods immediately prior to major UN summits on economic or social matters, the Expert Group holds a series of preparatory meetings during which it consults with various other bodies, including UN agencies, other intergovernmental organizations, and many NGOs. The aim is usually to formulate common African positions on key issues, and then to familiarize the other actors with these positions, so that by the time the summit itself occurs there will be a broad international consensus and the African demands can be more easily accommodated. This was the case, for instance, in the period preceding the World Summit on Social Development that took place in Copenhagen, Denmark, in March 1995. During that period, several Member States of the African Group transmitted written requests, via the Executive Secretariat, indicating the issues they would like to see the Expert Group include in the common African position. The Expert Group then used these requests to formulate the continent's economic and social demands that would be presented at the summit meeting.

However, the Expert Group does not necessarily limit itself only to economic and social matters. If the need arises, it can also constitute itself into an Expert Group on other matters, such as transportation, education, or deforestation, in order to develop proposals to be submitted to the plenary assembly. In such circumstances, it is usually the personnel responsible for the specific topic at the Permanent Missions of the Member States that would constitute the Expert Group. Thus, the specific individuals comprising the Expert Group during any meeting might depend on the specific topic being discussed at the time.

Chapter Twelve

Regional Coordinators

The Member States of the African Group at the UN are officially divided into five geographical regions of unequal size and weight. The regions are: West Africa (16 States), East Africa (12 States), Central Africa (10 States), Southern Africa (10 States), and North Africa (5 States). These internal divisions within the African Group result not only from geographical factors, but also from political, economic, and cultural considerations. Obviously, the circumstances faced by the States are not always identical across the continent, and certain issues might interest some States more than others. The problem of desertification, for instance, is likely to be of less interest to States in the equatorial region of Central Africa than to those in West Africa which are seriously affected by the expanding Sahara desert. Similarly, the Arab States of North Africa are not necessarily at the same level of economic development and do not face exactly the same social issues as many of those in the Sub-Saharan parts of the continent.

Consequently, each region has its own Coordinator, who is necessarily the Permanent Representative of one of the States in that region or another accredited diplomat. The Regional Coordinator is chosen by his counterparts in the region to serve for a defined term. Just as with the Chairmanship of the African Group, the position of Regional Coordinator rotates among the States in each region, following the alphabetical order of their names in English. However, the length of the term varies from one region to the next, often depending on the number of States in the region. In North Africa where there are only five States, for example, the Regional Coordinator serves a two-year term, while in West Africa, with sixteen States, the term lasts for only three months. One possible explanation for such a short mandate could be the fact that the States in that region wish to assign to the Coordinator only an administrative role and not a political one, since each Representatives might be inclined to serve the interests of his own State first and foremost. Another explanation could be the recognition that there are certain inherent political benefits to be derived from the post, and the States may wish to share those benefits more equitably among themselves.

The principal function of the Regional Coordinator is to serve as a channel of communication between the Member States of his region, on the one hand, and the various organs of the African Group, on the other. He is responsible for transmitting the demands of the States of his region to the decision-making bodies of the Group, and in return, to inform his Members of the decisions taken by the bodies. He is a full member of the Executive Committee and can sometimes participate in the work of the Committee on Candidatures in order to facilitate dialogue and communication among the Member States of his region.

In the example cited earlier of the choice of States to fill the seven Vice-President positions reserved for the African continent at the 1995 World Summit on Sustainable Development in Copenhagen, the Regional Coordinators played a very important role in the selection of candidates. In the case of the Southern African region, the States quickly arrived at a consensus and selected Zimbabwe as their candidate, thanks primarily to the diplomatic and negotiating skills of their Regional Coordinator who, at the time, was the Permanent Representative of Namibia. This can also give the impression that the Southern region is more cohesive than the other four regions. Conversely, the North African region, which is by far the smallest in terms of the number of States, sometimes displays much less cohesion. This is because Morocco, which withdrew in 1985 from the OAU and thus from the larger continental scene, usually tries to play a greater political role within the region and at the UN. This often results in clashes with other North African States.

However, the impact of the Coordinator is not necessarily limited to his region; his influence can extend to the other regions as well. For instance, he can persuade the other regions to withdraw their candidates and support the ones from his region, or he can accept to support the position of another region provided they agree to support his own region on another question. Personal diplomatic abilities can be a great asset for a Regional Coordinator, as a good diplomat can end up winning a lot of concessions not only for his region or his country, but also for himself.

Chapter Thirteen

The Welcome Committee

This is a group of very limited size and power, whose primary function is to organize receptions, dinner parties, and other formal and informal ceremonies for the African Group. The Welcome Committee usually springs to life when the Group is receiving a delegation from the AU's Executive Council, or when the Permanent Representative of one of the African States is getting ready to leave New York for another post.

The Committee is comprised essentially of personnel from the Executive Secretariat, which also provides most of the funding for the receptions. The main exception to this rule is when one of the African Permanent Missions to the UN undertakes to bear the costs. Sometimes, however, the African diplomatic missions are called upon to contribute financially or to send some of their staff to help organize the events.

The Chairman of the African Group always presides over the socio-cultural events organized by the Welcome Committee. Most of these are informal parties, but a few of them are formal ceremonies. For example, the 25th of May of each year, the anniversary of the signing of the OAU Charter, has been designated by the Group as Africa Day. During the festivities commemorating the occasion, the Welcome Committee always organizes a solemn ceremony including speeches, presentations, and other formal activities.

A good number of these ceremonies are held in the premises of the Libyan Permanent Mission to the UN, which has a huge reception hall and is located close to the UN Headquarters. The Libyan Mission has also proved willing on several occasions to bear the financial cost of staging these events. Obviously, Libya's Representatives can derive certain informal political benefits from this situation. For example, they can take advantage of the presence of so many foreign diplomats in their premises in order to exert some pressure, to solicit sympathy, or to gain assurances of support for Libya's political or diplomatic projects.

On rare occasions in the past these ceremonies were held in the OAU, which used to house the Executive Secretariat. However, the building lacked adequate facilities to host a large reception or a grand party. At other times, the ceremonies are held in the great reception halls at the UN Headquarters, but that makes them less private and not exclusive.

Chapter Fourteen

Ad Hoc Committees

These are small and short-lived committees with fixed mandates, created by the African Group to study specific issues. There are certain requirements that have to be met in order for an *ad hoc* committee to be created. Typically, this occurs when the African Group of the Whole identifies a specific problem that is of some importance to Africa, discusses it, but cannot find a quick or easy solution. In that case it authorizes its Chairman to request the Permanent Missions of a number of Member States to appoint experts or specialists from their countries to study the specific problem. These experts and specialists then constitute an *ad hoc* committee on that issue and are given a specified amount of time to examine it and report to the African Group. If the issue being studied by the new *ad hoc* committee is on the agenda of one of the UN bodies, then the committee will also be responsible for monitoring that UN body's treatment of the issue.

There is no limit to the size of an *ad hoc* committee of the African Group. That often depends on the question at hand and the number of Member States with readily available experts or specialist on the subject matter. The committee is usually called upon from time to time to brief the plenary assembly of the African Group on its progress. Here again, the regularity of the briefings depends on the specific mandate and duration of the committee. In some situations the committee is also mandated to draft a common African position on the issue under consideration, which may then be adopted by the African Group of the Whole.

The case of the Second United Nations Angola Verification Mission (UNAVEM II), whose mandate was supposed to expire on February 8, 1995, is a very good illustration of the way an *ad hoc* committee of the African Group is constituted and how it functions. Already on February 3, 1995, at the request of the Angolan delegation to the UN and upon the recommendation of the OAU's Council of Ministers, the African Group decided to seek to persuade the UN Security Council to not only renew UNAVEM's mission but also to expand it. The Group then created an *ad hoc* committee on the UNAVEM issue, and since at the time Nigeria was occupying one of the African seats on the Security Council, the Chairman of the African Group requested Nigeria to chair the *ad hoc* committee. The other Members who volunteered to serve on the committee were the Representatives of Kenya, Lesotho, Malawi, Tunisia, and, of course, Angola itself.

In a few days the *ad hoc* committee worked diligently on a strategy to secure the extension of the UN's peacekeeping operation in Angola. It met frequently to consider various drafts of a resolution that had as its centerpiece the transformation of UNAVEM II into an expanded UNAVEM III. All of the meetings were held at the OAU Building and the Executive Secretariat put all the necessary resources at the *ad hoc* committee's disposal in order to ensure success. The committee Members engaged in a lot of negotiations with the more influential States of the world, particularly the veto-wielding Permanent Members of the Security Council. In the end, they succeeded in drawing up a draft that was endorsed by the African Group of the Whole and, after some negotiation and a few modifications, it was unanimously adopted on February 8, 1995 by the UN Security Council (S/RES/976/1995). Thus was born the Third United Nations Angola Verification Mission (UNAVEM III), barely a few hours before the expiration of UNAVEM II. Thereafter, the *ad hoc* committee was disbanded.

Conclusion

From its uncertain beginnings in the early 1960s, the African Group has emerged today as one of the most dynamic and effective caucusing blocs at the United Nations. A cursory glance at the UN's weekly schedule of meetings in any given week is likely to give an indication of the frequency or meetings of the Group's various organs. The participation rate at these meetings is usually very high, and hardly ever is a meeting of one of the Group's organs cancelled for lack of a quorum. In fact, the African Group has become such a significant actor in international politics that most other actors, including other regional groups and some of the most powerful States, seek to win its approval and support before embarking on any major diplomatic course of action within the UN system.

At the institutional level, as these pages illustrate, the African Group has developed a complex structure of subsidiary organs that enable it to accomplish a number of tasks simultaneously (see Figure 1). There are certainly a number of positive and negative sides to this evolution. On the one hand, having a variety of specialized organs presents the advantage of making the Group more flexible and more efficient. The practice of letting its institutions evolve and develop as needed is a diplomatic asset that allows the African Group to adapt to any given context. For instance, the ability to create *ad hoc* committees allows it to react quickly to changing circumstances and to take account of unforeseen realities. An outside observer attending a meeting of any of the organs of the African Group at the UN cannot fail to be struck by the spirit of camaraderie that exists among the Representatives of the Member States. They express toward each other not only very much courtesy, but also a lot of warmth and brotherliness. Sometimes, the meetings of the plenary assembly have the feel of a great family reunion, and even when the

Representatives of different States disagree with one another, they remain
very polite and courteous. Oftentimes, the meetings take the appearance of
the famous palaver used to resolved disputes in many traditional African so-
cieties.

On the other hand, the lack of rigor and consistency in the way the Group
operates renders any analysis of its behavior very difficult. Although the ver-
sion of informal diplomacy practiced by the African Group is not very bu-
reaucratic, it tends to lend itself to inordinate verbosity, as each question, no
matter how controversial, has to be openly debated until a compromise is
reached. An untrained observer may easily leave one of the meetings with the
impression that the Group is long on rhetoric and short on action.

However, considering the number and the magnitude of the cleavages that
separated the three different groupings of African States prior to May 1963,
it seems remarkable that they succeeded in putting aside most of their differences and in establishing a cohesive caucusing group that has lasted for more
than 40 years now. It represents a concrete dimension of the Pan-African aspirations of the Founding Fathers of the OAU, who clearly desired to coordinate and harmonize the foreign policies and diplomatic strategies of their respective States as stated in Article II of the OAU Charter. In the discussions
leading up to the establishment of the OAU, the leaders expressed the need to
create among the Permanent Representatives of the African States at the UN
in New York, a regular and organized group that would serve as the continent's mouthpiece on matters of international politics within the UN framework (Amate 196-197; Addis Ababa Conference 13). Their dreams have
surely come true, as today the African Group at the UN is universally recognized as being the authentic representative of the aspirations of the African
peoples (Boutros-Ghali 30).

Finally, one more positive consequence of the success of the African Group
at the UN is that since 1963 it has become commonplace to create African
Groups at the various major diplomatic centers around the world where there
are large numbers of African diplomatic representatives. This is the case in
Geneva or Washington, for instance, where the heavy concentration of the
headquarters of international bodies makes it very logical for another African
Group to be set up to coordinate the States' diplomatic activities. It would be
interesting to undertake a comparative analysis of the functioning of the various African Groups at different locations, in order to see to what extent they
are similar or different, and also to what degree they might be influenced by
their respective venues. However, that is beyond the scope of the present
study.

Bibliography

"The Addis Ababa Conference." *Africa Report.* Vol. 8, No. 6. June 1963, p. 13.

Africa Report. Editorial. Vol. 8, No. 6, June 1963, p. 32.

"African Leaders Convene Rival Summits." *Africa Report.* Vol. 6, No. 1, January 1961, p. 11.

Amate, C.O.C. *Inside the OAU: Pan-Africanism in Practice.* New York: St. Martin's Press, 1986.

Andemicael, Berhanykun. *The OAU and the UN: Relations between the Organization of African Unity and the United Nations.* New York: African Publishing Co., 1976

Bailey, Sydney D. *The United Nations: A Short Political Guide.* London: Macmillan, 1989 (See Chapter 3: "Groups and Blocs").

Boutros-Ghali, Boutros. *Les difficultés institutionnelles du panafricanisme.* Geneva (Switzerland): Institut Universitaire des Hautes Études Internationales, 1971.

Chronologie politique africaine. 2e année, No. 1, janvier-février 1961a.

——. 2e année, No. 5, septembre-octobre 1961b, p. 2.

——. 4e année, No. 4, juillet-août 1963, pp. 2–3

——. 5e année, No. 2, mars-avril 1964, pp. 1–3.

——. 6e année, No. 1, janvier-février 1965, pp. 3–4.

Endeley, Isaac Njoh. *Le Groupe africain à l'ONU dans l'après-guerre froide.* Montréal: Université de Montréal, 1998. (Thèse de doctorat en science politique.)

Good, Robert C. "Four African Views of the Congo Crisis," *Africa Report.* Vol. 6, No. 6, June 1961, pp. 3–15.

Hippolyte, Mirlande. *Les États du Groupe de Brazzaville aux Nations unies.* Paris: Armand Colin, 1970.

Hoffman, Stanley. "In Search of a Thread: The UN in the Congo Labyrinth," in Norman J. Padelford and Rupert Emerson. "Africa and International Organization." *International Organization.* Vol. XVI, No. 2, Spring 1962, pp. 331–361.

Hovet, Thomas. *Bloc Politics in the United Nations.* Cambridge, MA: Harvard University Press, 1960.

"Internal Documents of the African Group at the UN." (Unpublished)

Kloman, Erasmus H. "African Unification Movements." in Norman J. Padelford and Rupert Emerson. "Africa and International Organization." *International Organization*. Vol. XVI, No. 2, Spring 1962 (pp. 387–404).

Marcum, John. "How Wide is the Gap Between Casablanca and Monrovia?" *Africa Report*. Vol. 7, No. 1, January 1962, pp. 3–18.

"Minutes of the Meetings of the African Group at the United Nations." (Unpublished)

"The Monrovia Conference." *Africa Report*. Vol. 6, No. 6, June 1961, p. 5

"Monrovia States Sign Charter in Lagos." *Africa Report*. Vol. 8, No. 2, February 1963, p. 17.

Newcombe, Hanna, and James Wert. *The Affinities of Nations: Tables of Pearson Correlation Coefficients of U.N. General Assembly Roll-Call Votes (1946–1973)*. Dundas, Ontario: Peace Research Institute, 1979.

New Zealand Ministry of Foreign Affairs and Trade. *United Nations Handbook*. Auckland, NZ: Manatu Aorere, 1996.

Nyangoni, Wellington. *Africa in the United Nations System*. Rutherford, NJ: Farleigh Dickinson University Press, 1985

Padelford, Norman J. and Rupert Emerson (Editors). "Africa and International Organization." *International Organization*. Vol. XVI, No. 2, Spring 1962.

Spencer, John H. "Africa at the UN: Some Observations." in Norman J. Padelford and Rupert Emerson. "Africa and International Organization." *International Organization*. Vol. XVI, No. 2, Spring 1962 (pp. 375–386).

S/RES/976/1995. United Nations Security Council Resolution 976, February 8, 1995.

Sterne, John R. L. "The Lagos Conference." *Africa Report*. Vol. 7, No. 2, February 1962, pp. 3–23.

"UAM Establishes New York Office." *Africa Report*. Vol. 7, No. 9, October 1962, page 30.

www.ingramcontent.com/pod-product-compliance
Lightning Source LLC
Chambersburg PA
CBHW021824270326
41932CB00007B/325